My Name is

Martha
*Motherf***ing*
Washington

By Dottie Pratt

This book contains monologues based on the officially recognized First Ladies of the United States of America. Any wives who died previous to a President's first election or who married a President after his final term ended, and any ladies who filled the role in lieu of Presidential wives when they couldn't or didn't want to, have been omitted.

This is a work of fiction. While based on real people, none of these monologues were said or written by any of these women. At least, I don't think they were... It'd be weird if they were, right?

Table of Contents

Martha Washington

Wife of George Washington
First Lady from 1789 to 1797

My name is Martha Motherfucking Washington. People got me all wrong. They think I'm dainty. They think I followed my husband from fort to fort during the war because I couldn't live without him. Truth is that bitch can't survive without me. "Martha, my feet are cold." "Martha, the French are making fun of my teeth." "Martha, my men are trying to mutiny." Without me taking care of him, the great General Washington would have been a weeping mess. And what thanks do I get? Instead of retiring and letting me take a fucking break, that fool becomes President of the United States, and I gotta be "Lady Washington," the goddamn hostess of fucking-shit-cunt-damn-fuck America. I'm too old for this shit.

Abigail Adams

Wife of John Adams
First Lady from 1797 to 1801

They call me Mrs. President and think I'll be offended. But what am I supposed to do? Sit quietly in the corner while my husband does all the interesting stuff? I don't think so! If John is going to ask my advice, I'm going to give it to him. Unofficially, of course, but that makes no difference to me. I do my motherly, wifely duties. I manage my household flawlessly. I take care of everyone's children in New York, Philadelphia, and the capital. And in my free time, if I just so happen to mention to my husband that in the new government women's rights should be guaranteed, slavery should end, and religion should stay separate from politics, I don't see a problem with that.

Dolley Madison

Wife of James Madison
First Lady from 1809 to 1817

Paul, come help me. Put down the napkins and come here. No, leave the china and come here! I'm sorry to raise my voice, Paul, but the British are on their way to burn Washington and this house to the ground and there are more important things to worry about than linens and plates. I need you to fetch a ladder so we can free this portrait of dear George. The Redcoats may humiliate us by taking our homes and comforts, but I'll be damned if President Washington has to watch them do it. Leave the silverware be! Dear Lord, how could I convince Republicans and Federalists to be civil to each other while having tea under this roof, but I cannot convince a servant to put down a fork?

Elizabeth Monroe

Wife of James Monroe
First Lady from 1817 to 1825

What people don't understand is how expensive being a politician's wife is. And I am wife to the most grandiose political post in this country. So people expect me to be grandiose and throw grandiose extravaganzas every night. But who's paying for these lavish events? My husband and I are from our own pockets. Why then should I be eschewed for wanting to host smaller, more intimate affairs? Why does everything in America have to be big and bold? Isn't elegance also a desirable attribute? Besides, the women in Washington have more fun boycotting my receptions than attending them anyway. Everyone would rather be at Dolley Madison's house being boisterous and merry. Harrumph. This never happened in France.

Louisa Adams

Wife of John Quincy Adams
First Lady from 1825 to 1829

We started in St. Petersburg. It's the kind of cold that, no matter how many layers you wear, it seeps past and invades your bones. Blinding white ice sprawls from your numb, frozen feet to every horizon, interrupted only by charred remnants of war-ravaged villages. Wooden crosses speckle the landscape. That land is not made for human habitation, yet everywhere you go... Orphans. Widows. Crippled men. Sometimes you sleep in the freezing carriage because it is more suitable than any houses in which to take shelter. Sometimes there are suitable houses, but the occupants will not allow you to enter, believing you to be of the same stock as those who destroyed their lives. We spent many evenings huddled together in the miserable, cold emptiness: making our way through winter.

Anna Harrison

Wife of William Henry Harrison
First Lady in 1841 *(his death)*

Dilsia, fold those things properly before packing them or I'll have your head. Put my hats in this trunk, not that one. And stop fussing over me. I feel fine. My illness is past. It's my husband, the goddamn President, who is now ill, and I need to get to goddamn Washington, D.C., to tend to him. Besides, it's not fair to make Jane bear my duties in perpetuity, no matter how desperately I wish to. Dilsia, what did I say about my hats? Dilsia? Where did she go? Oh, there you are. We need to finish this packing, chop chop. A telegraph? Thank you. *(opens telegraph, reads it, and sits in shock)* Dilsia, unpack my things. The President is dead.

Letitia Tyler

First Wife of John Tyler
First Lady from 1841 to 1842 *(her death)*

My dearest John. My life did not begin until I met you. I am so grateful you are by my side for the end of it. You've been away for so much of our marriage, I was afraid state business would keep you from me during my final days. I'm sorry my frail disposition has kept me from being a proper politican's wife to you, but Priscilla and Letty have much better social graces than I ever have. They'll never leave you in need of a female presence. My dearest John, I have two requests. The first, a rose. I wish for its fragrant beauty to escort me into eternity. Second, I want to see Elizabeth and Robert before I pass. The thought of never seeing my sister or son again breaks my heart. Please, John, make them come. I don't even need that rose. Just make them come.

Julia Tyler

Second Wife of John Tyler
First Lady from 1844 to 1845

It will be the grandest ball Washington has ever seen! Bunting over every wall. Flowers covering every inch of table space. Every lady should have a flower pinned to her bodice, along with tiny portraits of the President and, of course, myself. Priscilla and Letty will be beside themselves with disdain, but Dolley will think it brilliant. Speaking of my face, I want a representative from every newspaper from Maine to Florida in attendance. We'll begin the dancing with a series of "Julia Waltzes," but after that, every other dance should be a polka. And since this is the White House, and there should be a standard of elegance, have my coach ready with a team of matching white Arabian horses should I decide to make a grand exit at any moment. I might only be the First Lady for a few months, but, by God, I will be remembered.

Sarah Polk

Wife of James K. Polk
First Lady from 1845 to 1849

Hello. Happy Sabbath. No, I'm sorry, the President is not available for a meeting. After all, it's Sunday. Tell the British Minister that if he were a man of faith, he would choose a less holy day to meet my husband. But while I've got you here, can you please ensure there will be enough wine for tomorrow's dinner with the Cabinet and their wives? I want six different kinds. I'd like to hear them call me "Sahara Sarah" for my dry house after that. And please remember to set napkins this time. I don't want to deal with that ridicule again. If I can't trust my household staff to ensure there are napkins on the dinner table without me micromanaging them, then I have slaves in the yard that would love to do your jobs instead of theirs. Slaves who don't sneak liquor into my house or gamble after I go to bed. But don't fulfill these orders today. It's the Sabbath. Give today to the Lord. And God bless you.

Margaret Taylor

Wife of Zachary Taylor
First Lady from 1849 to 1850 *(his death)*

Dear God, thank you for all of the blessings you have bestowed upon my family and me. Thank you for my husband, even though he chose to run for this wretched presidency, which I begged you not to let him win. But I'm told you know what you're doing. Thank you for my children, especially Betty for taking over those tedious First Lady tasks. Surely it's a better course than me suffering through them. I cannot think of anything I've ever done that was so terrible you would sentence me to First Ladydom as penance. Thank you for my health, what little of it remains as I waste away my days in an invalid's chair. And thank you for this balmy, sticky, odorous summer day, which turns bathwater to sweat and sucks out everyone's will to live. In Jesus's name I pray, Amen.

Abigail Fillmore

Wife of Millard Fillmore
First Lady from 1850 to 1853

Did you know the White House has no library? What kind of house of reknown has no library? What kind of house has no library? I spent the majority of my youth in a two-room hovel, and even we had a section of the house reserved specifically for our books, which I always referred to as our library. The White House has three parlors, three dining rooms, a huge ballroom, but nowhere available to house important books. It's beyond my comprehension. There's a drawing room on the second floor that has no purpose except to be oval. That is where I'll put the books. Sophocles, Homer, Shakespeare, Dickens, Thackeray. They'll all have a place to stay in my White House.

Jane Pierce

Wife of Franklin Pierce
First Lady from 1853 to 1857

This was your fault! I asked you not to become a Senator, but you did anyway, and our first son died. I begged you not to imbibe in alcohol, but you did anyway, using the war as your excuse, and when you came back an alcoholic, our second son died. I pleaded and beseeched you not to accept the nomination for President, but you did anyway, and now our only remaining child — my only remaining son — is dead. God never wanted you to be a politician. How are you so blind to the signs? He tried so hard to dissuade you, but you never listened. Why didn't you listen? You killed our son! You killed them all!

Harriet Lane

Niece of James Buchanan
First Lady from 1857 to 1861

So what if my uncle never married? That gave him more time to focus on work. And I don't want to hear about those rumors about him and William King. That's total horseshit. Two married men can have a close bond and no one says anything of it, but two bachelors do the same thing and they have to be fucking? That's so stupid. Don't forget, my uncle was engaged in his youth. To a woman. It's not his fault she died. Besides, the duties a First Lady traditionally serves are actually much better suited to a younger woman. Why do you think so many presidents' wives have passed off those duties to their daughters and nieces? It takes a lot of energy to keep this place running right, and if there's one thing I'm proudly accused of having, it's my energy.

Mary Todd Lincoln

Wife of Abraham Lincoln
First Lady from 1861 to 1865 *(his death)*

I don't see what the big deal is. So I made some improvements to the White House. Believe me, it needed it. The house of the President should reflect the opulence of the position. That's all I did and everyone's biting my head off for it. It was bound to be expensive, but of course I have money to replace what I borrowed from the federal fund. Do you know how many men I convinced my husband to appoint to high-power positions? They owe me. I just need a little more time to collect those debts, and all will be right as rain. Just please — and this is really a request more for your benefit than for mine — please don't tell my husband.

Eliza Johnson

Wife of Andrew Johnson
First Lady from 1865 to 1869

All right, girls, let's go over the schedule for today. First, church. Then, Martha and Mary, you will host the Easter Egg Roll this morning. Mary will take care of logistics and Martha will entertain the wives and children. Mary, make sure your father actually talks to someone other than that wayward general, and make sure no one comes inside the house to bother me. Then, church. In the afternoon, I'll supervise preparations for Easter dinner while Martha attends the Washington Teachers Association's Easter luncheon and gives them my warm wishes. Mary, you take a nap. Then, church. Tonight, Martha will receive guests with your father while Mary watches the children upstairs. I'll come down after dinner to sit in the East Room and hope no one talks to me. Then, we'll all wash our faces, say our prayers, and go to bed. Any questions?

Julia Grant

Wife of Ulysses S. Grant
First Lady from 1869 to 1877

(cross-eyed) But Ulysses, I love it here. This has become more of a home to me than anywhere else ever was. This is where we belong. It's so much fun. The dinners, the receptions, the nights at the theater — just because Lincoln had bad luck with that last one doesn't mean you will. The country adores you. Why won't you seek a third term? Ulysses, look me in this eye. You know I can't percept whether you're telling the truth if you look in the other one. Please, Ulysses. Please, please, pleeeeease? You're the best president there ever was. All you have to do is say you want a third term and BOOM you'll have it. Then we can have a huge gala to celebrate. Ulysses, this eye. Look me in this eye.

Lucy Hayes

Wife of Rutherford B. Hayes
First Lady from 1877 to 1881

You don't need to have alcohol to throw a good party. There's only one thing you need: music. Piano at the start, strings and brass at the finish. I've been known to break out my guitar and join the band, and I have never needed a drop of liquid courage to do it. Also, it is essential to invite equal amounts of acquaintances and close friends so there will always be someone to turn to if conversation gets dull. But I'll let you in on the most indispensable hint; indoor plumbing has taken entertaining to whole new levels. No more long walks to privies outdoors. Just pop into an adjoining room, do your duties, and immediately return to the party. Not to mention, without alcohol, there are fewer of those trips, plus fewer brawls, fewer arguments, and fewer overnight guests who can't make their own ways home.

Lucretia Garfield

Wife of James Garfield
First Lady in 1881 *(his death)*

Excuse me? Am I hearing this correctly? Is there dis-crimination taking place under my own roof? Is Dr. Edson only working half as hard as the other doctors as they tend to my mortally wounded husband? Half the hours? Then why the hell is she making half the pay? I will not stand for this, and neither would my husband were he conscious. I don't want to bring this up, but I do have three sons actively practicing law whom I could have draw up discrimination lawsuits immediately to fight this wrong. But it needn't come to that. Dr. Edson is just as capable as the other doctors tending my husband or else she would not be here. Therefore, pay her what is owed to her. Now.

Caroline Harrison

Wife of Benjamin Harrison
First Lady from 1889 to 1893

When we moved into the White House I did not realize we were going to share our rooms with rats, spiders, and cockroaches. And silly me was convinced that all of the toilets in the house would actually flush, instead of just the ones downstairs. And could someone tell me why every other government building in Washington has had electricity installed but the White House is still dependent on gas and candles? It really is a mystery to me how so many families could have come and gone in this house without noticing any of these issues before I did. Maybe I've just grown accustomed to such lavish luxuries, coming from the backwaters of Indiana, but I really think we could do better here.

Frances Cleveland

Wife of Grover Cleveland
First Lady from 1886 to 1889, and again from 1893 to 1897

Ah! It is good to be home. Oh, look at this new wallpaper. That's...nice. And I see we've got new rugs. Mmmmmmmm great. But Grover, look. *(flips a switch)* Electricity! That would have come in handy during our wedding. Looks like the staff believed me when I told them we'd be back in four years. They took excellent care of this place for us. It's still the good old house I remember. Maybe we can actually live here this time and not have to rent a private place outside town? I'm sure the media's interest in "Frank, the President's Young Bride" has waned. We're an old married couple now. No? Well, there's no harm in asking. I'll still insist on having my Saturday morning receptions here with the working women of Washington, no matter how much you'd rather sleep in, my love. Washington, the Clevelands are back!

Ida McKinley

Wife of William McKinley
First Lady from 1897 to 1901 *(his death)*

I was very well-travelled in my youth. I wasn't always confined to a chair. Oh, William, it's all right, it's not like this chair is a secret. But as I was saying, I came upon a series of paintings in Europe which caught my eye because the brush strokes were nothing like I'd ever seen. I went to meet the painter, and imagine my surprise when I walked into the room, ready to shake his hand, only to discover he had no hand to shake. No arms or legs either. He had taught himself to paint while holding a brush in his mouth... *(has a seizure)* Anyway, the thought of that painter has stuck with me. Even after my illnesses led me to this chair, I remembered him and all of his accomplishments, and I knew, so long as I'm alive, I can be as active as I choose to be.

Edith Roosevelt

Wife of Theodore Roosevelt
First Lady from 1901 to 1909

Oh, Teedie. I love these morning hours we have together. No kids, no politics. By the way, I think your idea of inviting Booker T. Washington to dinner is the best idea you've ever had. Oh, Teedie. I don't think I could function without this regular time spent alone with you. Your energy revives me. By the way, the children mentioned taking a trip to Europe while you're visiting the territories and I highly support the idea. Oh, Teedie. You are so powerful and strong and courageous. You are every definition of a man. By the way, I wish you would stop dismissing the Secret Service men I've assigned to watch over you. I will not have you meeting the fates of McKinley, Garfield, and Lincoln. Oh, Teedie. I am so lucky to have you as my husband. Now go, I have work to do.

Helen Taft

Wife of Howard Taft
First Lady from 1909 to 1913

Votes for Women! Votes for Women! Oh, hello. Why, yes, I am Nellie Taft. Why would you be surprised to see me here? I'm as active a suffragette as anyone. Votes for Women! If a woman can demonstrate at least a general knowledge of political issues and candidates, she should be able to vote. The same requirement should be held for men as well. If a man doesn't know what's going on politically and a woman does, it makes absolutely no sense that he may vote in an important election while she is forbidden. Votes for Women! I could never convince my husband to support our movement, and I couldn't be too vocal about our cause during his presidency, but today is the last day of that era, so now I can do whatever I damn well please. If you'll excuse me, there's a demonstration going on. Votes for Women!

Ellen Wilson

First Wife of Woodrow Wilson
First Lady from 1913 to 1914 *(her death)*

Good morning, Doctor. How am I feeling? Like my kidneys are so inflamed that they're killing me. Oh wait, that's actually happening. *(laughs)* At least I haven't lost my sense of humor, right? Doctor, there is something I wanted to discuss with you this morning. I can feel myself fading. I know the end is near. I don't want to burden my husband with any extra stress during my...you know. My slums project will never get off the ground without me backing it, so I won't make him promise to see it through. But after I'm gone, after he's had a chance to let it affect him the way a widower needs to be affected, I want you give him this message. I hope he marries again. I'd hate for him to be lonely on my account. That's all. Oh, wait, Doctor. Please, take care of my husband.

Edith Wilson

Second Wife of Woodrow Wilson
First Lady from 1915 to 1921

Just a minute! I'll be right there. *(peeking head out door)* Hello, Mr. Secretary. I'll take those papers to the President. No, I'm sorry, you can't see him. He's not feeling well. But I'll certainly help him go over these papers and get back to you on the matters he feels up to tackling. Okay, bye. What? So what if it's been weeks since you saw him? I told you, he's ill. He's not up to visitors. But he's plenty up to working, so if you don't mind... *(cannot close the door)* You're insistent on seeing him, aren't you? *(looks into room)* Darling, the House Secretary insists on seeing you. *(deeper voice)* Did you tell him I'm ill? *(her voice)* Of course, but he insists. *(deeper voice)* Very well. Give me a minute. *(her voice, out the door)* Just give us a minute. *(closes door, rushes to bed, struggles to set President to sitting position, rushes back to door, and opens it wide for a split second before bringing it back to almost closed)* There, you've seen him. Now off with you. We've all got work to do. *(closes door and exhales breath of relief)*

Florence Harding

Wife of Warren G. Harding
First Lady from 1921 to 1923 *(his death)*

I am riding a train. I am riding a train with my husband. He is right next to me, but I do not know whether he knows I am here. I have been a single mother. I have been a newspaper editor. I have been betrayed by the one I loved the most. I have been the recipient of blackmail. I have been a campaigner. I have been a strategist. I have been a supporter. I have been a boycotter. I have been the First Lady to the President of the United States of America. I have been a survivor. Now I am a widow. Now I must somehow survive this. I am riding a train. I am riding a train with my husband right next to me.

Grace Coolidge

Wife of Calvin Coolidge
First Lady from 1923 to 1929

I'm here! Is that not enough? I am the First Lady, and the First Lady is expected to be here, so I am here. Every other woman in the world would be granted a reprieve at a time like this, but not me. I am indentured to this public life, and everything I do is scrutinized by the media, and there's not one thing I can do about it. I'd rather be anywhere but here. At home, taking a hot bath. Cheering the Red Sox until I'm hoarse. Bawling my eyes out over the fresh grave of my son. But I am here. And I will go back out there in full view of the public, and no one will know this little outburst ever occured because I am the First Lady of the United States. Whether I want to be or not.

Lou Hoover

Wife of Herbert Hoover
First Lady from 1929 to 1933

Oh, look at this! What a remarkable-looking device. What is it called? A movie camera? How extraordinary. I've seen filming cameras before, of course, but none so portable as this. I can hold it in one hand. Incredible. Show me how it works. Look through here. Oh, I can see you right there. Am I filming you now? How do I start? Push this button. There, I've caught you. Wowee, the rocks I could film with this. It does make the room look a tad different than I know it actually looks. It must be the apertures adjusting the focal length and and reacting with my crystalline lens to marginally distort the visual field and display the optimal plane of sight. What a fun little machine. I'll take it!

Eleanor Roosevelt

Wife of Franklin Delano Roosevelt
First Lady from 1933 to 1945 *(his death)*

I was not made for a life of servitude and social engagements. The thought of being First Lady as the position has always been served depresses me. I cannot be a mere backdrop for my husband. I am an independent creature. I have been a stand-in for Frank since he started his campaign for the White House, so how the hell am I supposed to dissolve into the background now that he's here? I have a voice. I have a mind. I will speak it and I will be heard. I should be able to support publicly the issues important to me. If I disagree with my husband's platforms, I should be able to say so. I am not content to decorate and socialize and organize banquets. I am not the most charming person in the world, but I will not be America's wallflower. My name is Eleanor Roosevelt, and you will know I am here.

Bess Truman

Wife of Harry S. Truman
First Lady from 1945 to 1953

Let's see. What am I supposed to do today? "Breakfast with the Cabinet wives." I don't wanna do that. "Press conference." I am not doing that. "Visit Red Cross." I'll do that. "Luncheon to support Washington Animal Rescue League." Will any animals be there? No animals? Then I don't wanna do that. "Pick out china for First Lady collection." I suppose I've put that off long enough...but I can put it off longer. "Interview with—" You know I don't do interviews. I never have and I never will. But I'll tell you what. I'll do the breakfast if you forget about the interview. Deal? Deal. Is that it? Then I'm off to Harry's office for the day. What's that? Oh, yes, the breakfast. *(big sigh)* I'm going, I'm going.

Mamie Eisenhower

Wife of Dwight D. Eisenhower
First Lady from 1953 to 1961

Who doesn't like pink? It's cheerful, pretty, feminine. It brightens up any garden, room, or outfit. Have you ever heard the phrase "the pink of perfection"? Well, I think pink *is* perfection. There's nothing that a dash of pink can't improve. It's a dreary, rainy day? Add a pink umbrella. You're sad and can't get out of bed? Put on a pink outfit and I guarantee your mood will improve. There is a lot of darkness in the world. It can be a very hard place for a lot of people. It has become my mission to bring cheer wherever I go. I have found the simplest and most effective way to do that is: pink.

Jackie Kennedy

Wife of John F. Kennedy
First Lady from 1961 to 1963 *(his death)*

Come here, John. Let's put on your coat. You look dapper in your little suit. The spitting image of your father. Now listen, John. This is very imporant. You may hear people say mean-sounding things about your father. Most of them will not be true. It's important you remember that. He wasn't always the most loyal husband to me, but he was a wonderful father to you and your sister. And he was a magnificent president. We're going to the moon because of him. You should always be proud of who your father was, no matter what anyone might say about him. Is that a promise, John? All right, my darling. Let's go say goodbye to Father.

Lady Bird Johnson

Wife of Lyndon B. Johnson
First Lady from 1963 to 1969

Gentlemen of Congress. Howdy. I come before you today to point out something everyone seems to have ignored for a long time; this country looks a mess. When my husband was vice president, I had the privilege of travelling to thirty-three different countries, and the only places we visited that did not uphold the natural beauty and grace of their countries were the ones recently ravaged by war. What does that say about us? I'm from a small town in east Texas, and in Texas we're taught to take pride in our appearance. It's not a matter of vanity, but a matter of putting your best foot forward. I have created the First Lady's Committee for a More Beautiful Capital to return this city to the beautiful place it should be, and I hope to expand this initiative to include the entire country. After all, if we let our land fall to shambles, then what the heck are we fighting for?

Pat Nixon

Wife of Richard M. Nixon
First Lady from 1969 to 1974 *(his resignation)*

What a lot of people don't know about Dick is he and I share a love of the theatre. In fact, that's how we met. We were cast in the same community production of *The Dark Tower*. He asked me on a date, and on that very date, he asked me to marry him. What a nut! As dramatic as marrying a man after one date would have been, I was not the kind of woman who went around throwing her ring finger away to anyone. At that time, I had plenty of gentlemen paying attention to me and I wasn't quite ready to give that up. But he was fun and ambitious and persistent, as the country well knows about him now. We became very good friends. He'd even give me rides to and from dates with other men. After two years of torturing him, I finally relented. I have been the happiest woman in the world ever since.

Betty Ford

Wife of Gerald R. Ford
First Lady from 1974 to 1977

Fucking Nixon just had to go and resign. Now I'm stuck here in this fucking house just waiting for Gerry's fucking term to be over. When that blessed day comes, I'm gonna tap dance with joy all over the fucking Cabinet room's conference table. I swear, if that man runs for re-election — or rather for first election if we're being honest — I'm gonna consider leaving his ass. With this breast cancer diagnosis coming at the worst fucking time, the last thing I need is to be First fucking Lady. They say stress leads to cancer, and with the stress of that job, before you know it I'll have cancer growing in the other boob. I just want to go back to Michigan. Is that so much to ask? It's times like this I would give anything for a fucking drink.

Rosalynn Carter

Wife of Jimmy Carter
First Lady from 1977 to 1981

Some fella had the nerve to tell me that a woman's place is in the home and that's all. Perhaps that was once the culture in America, but not anymore. I have no intention of being confined. My Jimmy is the President, but I am his equal in every way except job title. He tells me everything he talks about in Cabinet meetings anyway, so I'm gonna go to those Cabinet meetings and hear the facts myself. Jimmy is a very busy man, so I'm gonna travel in and outside of this country as his envoy. It'll be like he's in two places at once. And since I'll know as much relevant information as he does, and I know that man to his core, I know what he would answer to any question I come across. Tell me, if I have the ability and desire to do all that, what good would I be "in the home and that's all"?

Nancy Reagan

Wife of Ronald Reagan
First Lady from 1981 to 1989

Hi, Joan. I don't have much time to talk, so I just need some yes's and no's about the stars' positions for Ronnie's safety. I wanted to confirm about his address to Congress tomorrow at 9:15. Will Ronnie be shot? No? So still the same as the last time we talked. I know the stars don't change that quickly, Joan, but I need to be safe. There's talk of a family trip to Camp David. If we leave Friday morning and return Sunday evening, will Ronnie be shot? No? Excellent. For his trip to France next week, you told me the best time for takeoff is 1:52 am Eastern time. But Joan, at any point during the flight, will Ronnie be shot? Why are you hesitating? That's it. I'm cancelling the trip. Okay, Joan, that's all the questions I have for today. You're a life saver. I'll talk to you again soon. Take care.

Barbara Bush

Wife of George H.W. Bush
First Lady from 1989 to 1993

Today I want to talk about literacy. I know that's what I talked about yesterday and what I'll talk about tomorrow. I've discussed the cause with everyone including Oprah and yet it is still a huge issue. Millions of Americans cannot read beyond a fourth-grade level, and millions more can barely read English at all. I know we can do something about this, as much as I know my hair is whiter than snow and my skin is more wrinkled than a bloodhound's rear in cold water. Whether it takes free community literacy classes or perhaps government literature that progresses in reading level as the writing goes on, there's gotta be something. I just published a children's book, and I will not rest until everyone in this country is able to read and enjoy the story of my dog Millie's puppies.

Hillary Rodham Clinton

Wife of Bill Clinton
First Lady from 1993 to 2001

I've had a lot of firsts as a First Lady. I was the first First Lady to graduate from law school. I was the first First Lady not to take my husband's last name after marriage. The only reason I eventually did is because Bill got into politics in Arkansas, and it was more politically savvy for his wife to share his last name. I was the first First Lady to have the same level of political acumen as my husband. When he was elected President, America sort of got two presidents for the price of one. I was the first First Lady to have an office in the West Wing. I was the first First Lady to chair a presidential task force. I was also the first First Lady to be ruthlessly investigated by Congress, but I hold no ill will. When my husband completes his second term, I'll become the first First Lady to run for a Senate seat. After that, heaven only knows what other firsts I'll accomplish.

Laura Bush

Wife of George W. Bush
First Lady from 2001 to 2009

What about the people, George? The people did nothing wrong. Yes, there are bad folks in the Middle East doing very bad things, attacking our American sanctity, but it's not the entire Middle East. We can't go to war with entire nations of innocent children, women, and men who have nothing to do with what happened to us. If you do this, you have to be specific. Go to war against al-Qaeda. Go to war against the Taliban. Go to war against the bad folks, George. Leave the good ones alone. They've gotta know we're on their side just as much as we're against the people also making their world hell. You're a good man, George. Remember that when you make your decision about what to do.

Michelle Obama

Wife of Barack Obama
First Lady from 2009 to 2017

I am a strong woman. I have raised my daughters to be strong women. I have worked hard for every single thing I have, and I am proud of my life. My goal is to encourage others to be strong. But for one to be strong, you've got to be healthy. Don't feed your body. Fuel it. Get up and move every single day. If you keep those muscles and bones moving, they'll be able to go on for years and years and years. This is how my family lives. This is how America should live. Respect yourself enough to take care of yourself. Be strong. Be healthy. If I can get just ten percent of this country to live healthier, I will consider my life a success.

Melania Trump

Wife of Donald J. Trump
First Lady from 2017 to *???*

I am a strong woman. I have raised my son to be strong. I have worked hard for everything I have...and I'm proud...
(breaking down) I have worked hard. I work hard not to say how I really feel. It is so hard to pretend you support one thing when you believe something completely different. But if I didn't pretend, I'd lose everything. I'm a joke. What kind of a role model is that for my son? Of course I don't want to take him into Washington, into the middle of the madness. Away from there, I can keep him safe. I can keep him good. *(pulling herself together)* I am a strong woman. I have worked for everything I have.

ABOUT THE AUTHOR

Dottie Pratt received Bachelors of Arts in Theatre Production and Creative Writing from Georgia College & State University. She works as a freelance copy editor (deathtotypos.com) and previously published the one-person play, *...And Then He Kissed Me*. She resides in Salt Lake City with two needy cats and constant cravings for jellybeans.